Friends With Benefits

Rethinking Friendship, Dating and Violence

SHAHLA KHAN

The information in this book is meant to supplement, not replace, proper violence prevention training. The author and publisher advise readers to take full responsibility for their safety and know their limits. Before practicing the skills described in this book, be sure that you are in control and comfortable, and do not take risks beyond your level of experience, aptitude, training, and comfort level.

TRIGGER WARNING

This book contains sexual references, strong language and incidences of rape and sexual violence that some readers may find upsetting.

AGE WARNING

Material may not be suitable for people under 16 years.

DEDICATION

To all survivors of violence and those who stood for them,
known and unknown.

CONTENTS

ACKNOWLEDGMENTS

Although a book has only a certain number of words but it conceals a lifetime of experiences and encounters with people that leave impressions on us. I would like to thank all my male friends who made me believe that men are capable of sharing and caring for women without objectification. I also want to thank all my female friends who stood by me when I needed and guided me in their own beautiful and quirky ways.

Section 1

About This Book

1
WHAT IS FRIENDS WITH BENEFITS

Friends With Benefits is a crash course in adult sex education that unifies humankind against gender based violence.

It is no news to you and me that in this generation more than half of the events in our daily news consist of violent crimes the majority of which are sex crimes and/or gender based violence. When I say gender based crimes, the statistics point more towards women as victims but men are certainly not excluded. These crimes affect both men and women although disproportionately.

Sex education that some of you might have received in high school may be informative on the human reproduction system and STDs. However, sex education must not stop there at school. In the age we live, from video games to advertising, every single message we read, hear or watch has an impact on us. The hyper-sexualization of women and sadly, children, the violence portrayed in video games, the objectification of bodies and the false perceptions of masculinity are just to name a few things that effect us.

Without us noticing, they change our perceptions. For instance, a young girl who reads *Glamour* Magazine may instantly feel that she is not beautiful enough. Focusing on the perceptions of aggressive and violent sex portrayed in films, media and books, our generation has become extremely violent and the meaning of sex has changed.

While sex is supposed to be a shared connection, an experience enjoyed by two mutually consenting adults, it has now become more of a master-slave thing where one person is an object used by the other person for sexual gratification (which is not mutual).

This book aims to remind you, the reader, that sex

and sexual crime are two absolutely different things. Sex is a beautiful connection of intimacy and feeling cared for. Gender based violence including crimes of sexual nature are at the end of the day crimes for which **no one but the criminal is responsible.**

Most importantly, this book will help you connect with people in a platonic way so you can explore the possibilities of human connections beyond sex. People who wish you to be safe in the face of danger and who help you heal after a trauma.

The content of this book is precise and short on purpose. The motive is mainly to inform you and make you think and question what is being taught to us in everyday life. Instead of taking things at face value, I want you to understand that you are free to make your own new rules and explore life in your own way. And I don't want you to spend years reading a book instead of exploring a life full of surprises and adventures.

2
WHY DO WE NEED FRIENDS WITH BENEFITS

In this age of fear and crime, when every message you hear warns you in some way about how insanely capable people are of committing crimes and hurting you, this book is a breath of fresh air.

As Dr. Megan McElheran says in her TED talk, human beings are intrinsically social. There is also no denying that there are people in this world who can hurt you. Life can be unfair to good people sometimes and events beyond our control can leave us devastated.

I do however feel that there are other people in this very same world, who are kind and wish us well. People who hold our hand through the worst times and take a stand for us when we seem to be crippled.

These can be members of the family, friends, relatives, acquaintances or strangers. Dr Megan says that there is no psychological treatment or therapy that can heal a traumatized person better than a human connection.

> Friendship is the underlying element, the common denominator of every relationship.

Like several other academics, I completely agree with her theory and therefore found the basis of this book. The human connection which she speaks about in lay man terms is friendship. Friendship is the underlying element, the common denominator of every relationship.

The best father, mother, teacher, sibling is the one in whom you see a 'friend'. People you feel comfortable around and share the big and small details of your life with.

While commonly accepted 'benefits' of friendship are sexual in nature, I want you to broaden that thought pattern and include other benefits like care, compassion, empathy and faith. Sharing those benefits with not just one single person but among a small group of individuals.

Fighting gender based crimes can be much easier when we scrub off the word 'gender' and call it crimes against our friends. Not one person on earth is immune to crime and trauma. It is simply beyond our control. What we can control is our behavior, our social connections and the way we allow others to look out for us while we look out for them.

> Not one person on earth is immune to crime and trauma.

The book is therefore divided into three parts for sake of simplicity. The first part is dedicated to friendship; making friends and being friendly. It also digs deeper into the science of social isolation and its impacts on the human psyche. You will also discover how to know if a person will prove to be a good friend and how you can be friends with the opposite gender without fuss.

The second section of this book is dedicated to healthy dating habits. Being in a relationship begins with yourself. The science and art of happy relationships begin with the way you see and treat yourself. You will learn about positive sexuality and self confidence in this ever demeaning world of advertisements and judgments coming from the society. You will also learn the pros and cons of random dating aka hook up culture and ponder whether or not it is for you. Healthy dating and sexual desires need sexual values. You make your own based on your beliefs and never change them to please someone.

> Technology has changed the world we interact with each other hence the assault is not limited to physical anymore.

In the third section of this book, I discuss the aggressive and violent side of sex and relationships. Technology has changed the world we interact with each other hence the assault is not limited to physical anymore. You will learn what you can do when you are not the victim or the perpetrator. You will also discover what consent and blurred lines actually mean. No matter what background, race, religion or gender, you will learn how to react to assault, how to get or offer help and support without passing judgment and the impacts of alcohol and porn addiction on those around you.

There is a lot more but I will leave you to it to discover the rest.

I hope this book will help you grow and mature emotionally.

In friendship,

Shahla

3
WHO IS FRIENDS WITH BENEFITS FOR

This book is for people

A. Who believe in the safety and wellbeing of themselves and that of others

B. Who want to explore what violence instilled trauma can do to people

C. Who are not afraid to make their own rules

D. Who believe in the power and sweetness of social connections

E. Who do not classify themselves as sexists, racists, ageists etc

There are two kinds of extremes for whom this book may not be very useful.

In case you don't know, a misogynist is a person who is strongly prejudiced against women. If you are one, you may not learn much from this book because this book is intended to create equality and animosity between human beings regardless of their genders.

If you are an advanced level feminist and are already an advocate of gender equality, there is a slight possibility that many arguments of this book may not be new to you. The information in this book is introductory level intended for young people who are unaware of these topics and need a beginners lesson to take a leap in favor of gender equality.

Section 2

Make Friends

4
MAKE NEW RULES

Begin with making new rules about friendship and its benefits. I am damn sure until now every time you heard the phrase 'Friends With Benefits' it meant two people acting like friends who are also involved in a casual sexual relationship.

My suggestion: **erase that pattern of thinking from your mind.**

Make friends with anyone around you. If you have common interests or like each other's company, you can certainly chose to spend more time with them and hang out more often. When it comes to benefits though, make sure that the benefits are things like:

- Looking out for each other
- Standing up when required
- Sharing troubles without gossiping about them, etc

> *You don't have to sleep with every friend you have.*

You must know that the sexual element is absolutely a choice. You don't have to sleep with every friend you have.

Many people argue that boys and girls can never be friends. They always end up getting attracted toward one another; casually pursue that attraction and then one falls in love with another and that leads to heart breaks and arguments.

You may know what works best for you. But there are ways to ensure that your friendship stays intact. For instance, don't make just one friend rather a small group of 3 or 4 people that hang out together. That way you wouldn't be hanging out with just one person.

I also feel that people who say that boys and girls cannot be friends have a very limited vision of the world and probably have issues with self control and decision making.

We need to expand the definition of Friends With Benefits. Why should the benefit of friendship only be sexual? Why can't it be looking out for each other, calling to see if your friend has reached home safely, asking if your friend needs help expressing his emotions, if one friend in the group can remain sober during a party to ensure everyone is safe? One might argue that these benefits are inherent in friendship anyways and do not need to be called 'benefits'.

I disagree. Not every friend is going to care to that extent. Just like sleeping with a friend is a **deal** that you make outside the realms of friendship, why not expand the deal and include: emotional support, guard and vigilance in times of danger?

5
BEING LONELY VS BEING FRIENDS

At some points in life when someone we trust hurts us badly, we jump to the conclusion that we must never make friends again. It isn't just about friends, but also applies to relationships.

> *Loneliness and the feeling of being unwanted is the most terrible poverty.*
> - **Mother Teresa**

When this happens, we isolate ourselves from the entire world and create our own little world. Thanks to the internet, we stay under the illusion that we are connected to the world. Sadly we aren't.

Apart from the breaking of trust, when we finish school and move to university life or change jobs, we often find ourselves as the 'new guy/girl' in town. This being new experience can be daunting. You may miss your old friends, your hangout places and activities and this may stop you from making new relationships.

> *Negative emotions like loneliness, envy, and guilt have an important role to play in a happy life; they're big, flashing signs that something needs to change.*
>
> - **Gretchen Rubin**

We all react differently to different situations. But studies suggest that over 40% of adults suffer from loneliness in their lifetime – young adults being particularly vulnerable - and research shows that direct loneliness impacts our physical health as much as cigarette addiction!

There can be other reasons why we get isolated. May be we don't look a certain way or speak in a certain accent or even language. We might have different values, cultural background or religion.

We may feel people don't like us based on our own assumptions or experiences.

While there will always be someone who may dislike you, there are others who will like you for who you are. The best thing about friendship is that it surpasses the differences and binds two people like two peas in a pod.

Making friends and spending quality time is a 'health' choice you make for your emotional, psychological and even physical wellbeing. Calamities of loneliness include:

- Reduced life span
- High/low blood pressure
- Clinical depression
- Suicidal thoughts
- Sleep disturbances
- Hostility and violence

- Decline in mental abilities
- High cholesterol and BMI
- Increase in stress hormones
- Rapid progression of Alzheimer's disease

One of the critical negative outcomes of loneliness is that it makes us overly critical about ourselves. We judge and over analyze everything we do which leads to a steep fall in our self esteem. We loathe ourselves and feel others do too.

> *Pray that your loneliness may spur you into finding something to live for, great enough to die for.*
> **Dag Hammarskjold**

Therefore, you know now that happy and healthy relationships are the backbone of human life and prosperity. But before we begin counting our relationships, it is important to take note of our friends. Every single relationship on the planet is based on friendship. If your mother for instance is like a friend who shares your gossips and chuckles along without judgment and lecture, you have a really healthy and nurturing relationship. On the other hand, no matter how big your family is and no matter how many siblings you have, if they don't talk to you, share your problems and laughs, you are lonely.

I used to think that the worst thing in life is to end up all alone, it's not. The worst thing in life is to end up with people who make you feel alone.

- **Robin Williams**

6
GIRL CODE VS GUY CODE VS HUMAN CODE

Now that we have established the importance of social bonds aka friendship in our lives, let us move a step further to cross gender friendships.

> *I find it easier to claim that I am friends with a monkey rather than with a man.*

Friendship is a relationship that can be between any two living creatures on the planet, even with animals.

Surprisingly, it is easier to claim that a monkey is my friend but harder to claim that a boy is my friend. May be because it takes the guess work out.

That is simply because for some reason, our society does not tend to agree that men and women can be friends. When guys meet guys and do their thing, whether it is sports or beer, it is said to be sharing camaraderie and bonding. They stay loyal to each other, laugh on common jokes, complain about women and play by this rule called the 'guy code'. The **'guy code'** implies their loyalty and commitment towards the males of the group.

Girls have a similar friends circle where they meet up, gossip, share laughs, common jokes, activities they love, pretty much everything that men do. They do follow a similar commitment and loyalty rule called the **'girl code'** where by a girl respects other girl's boundaries and many such things.

Looking at the picture from far, it does not seem too different to me. While we make a commitment to protect and respect the members of our gender, why don't we extend it to all genders?

> *The greatest healing therapy is friendship and love.*
> **- Hubert H. Humphrey, Jr.**

We, the westerners have somehow never questioned our age old culture where we stereotype the opposite gender. There are certain ways in which we always think of the person of the other gender: pretty, beautiful, handsome, she can be just friends, or we are always going to be good as colleagues. Our societies and communities would do much better if you could think on the grounds of humanity first and get over the attitude of being a typical sexist. Men are not from Mars and women are not from Venus instead we are all people. Each having some potential that needs to be explored.

Why is it Necessary for Us to See Each Other as Equals

If we were only to get our minds off gender wars we would achieve much more than what we have gained. Our societies would be free of vices like sexual harassment, and gender based biases and discrimination. People would feel much more secure and they would not have to fend themselves of the opposite gender all the time instead they would use their energies to engage in something far more productive.

Exploring the Potential in National Resources

We are not just people but for our economy we are human resources and before we invest in the betterment of our society we need to get our attitude right or all our money would simply be going down the drain. We need all our members to be going in the right direction to be working hard to achieve what they want in their lives instead of taking the easy way out. We can help each other perform better only by having the right attitude i.e. by thinking of us as equal members of the society rather than anything else. We have wasted enough by thinking of each other as gender born to fulfill a single purpose. Now we need to overcome the way we see each other as aliens and we need to act as human before anything else.

> *Men are not from Mars and women are not from Venus instead we are all people from Earth.*

The common GOALS

Men and women may be different biologically and in many other ways. But guess what? On the very basic level we want the same things from life? Remember Maslow's Hierarchy of needs???

Maslow did not make two different pyramids, one for men and one for women. He did not differentiate in identifying what men want and what women want. Why, you ask? Well that is because they both need the same things!!!

Same needs and wants make us equals on most levels despite our differences. Can't we focus on those similarities and learn to survive as co species and stop regarding the opposite sex as aliens? You need to know that this is possible by simply changing your perspective. Beginning to look at the other gender as a human and foster friendship, simple and pleasant.

> *Maslow did not make two different pyramids, one for men and one for women. He did not differentiate in identifying what men want and what women want.*

7

TOUGH LOVE- THE UNWELCOME
BENEFIT OF FRIENDSHIP

A friend is the one who is true to your face even if it means hurting your feelings sometimes. Especially when it comes to grown partners and intimate relationships. Most of the times, our family and friends see what we don't see or are just too scared to admit.

When my sister announced her first engagement, not only was the family unhappy, her friends too tried to persuade her to change her decision. People knew the guy too well and knew his intentions. The sad but natural reaction to this situation is denial. And it is not just her, most people react that way; men and women. When their friends try to convince them that they may be with the wrong person, they snap out and blame their friends that they are jealous.

While there is no doubt that some people may be jealous, not all people would dare to come to your face and try to warn you. It is very natural for us all to think that **'I am finally with the other half of my life'** because it is what we want to believe in. Isn't this the happy ending of every romantic comedy from *Cinderella* to *Pretty Woman* that we were all promised?

> *Support your friends – even in their mistakes. But be clear, however, that it is the friend and not the mistake you are supporting.*
> **- Hugh Prather**

It is dreamy and seductive and out of the world but from a realist's perspective, it is just one part of the story. Your friends know you well and they warn you for your betterment.

I have a friend who I know since 3rd grade. Before she got married, we were chatting about her wedding plans and she casually mentioned that the groom and his family made her sign that she won't ever work after marriage. I was curious to know why that was. She said that's because they are very posh, filthy rich and they don't want their daughter in law to work. And also she didn't want to work.

> *Choose your friends wisely-they will make or break you.*
> **- J. Willard Marriott**

I responded cautiously and warned her that whether she wants to work or not must be her personal choice. A groom and his family who are trying to control such basic decisions of her life before the wedding would surely turn nasty after it. Despite my warning, she did not take it seriously and went ahead. The marriage lasted twelve months by when she got beaten up and finally divorced.

Tough love is a basic element of friendship and you must be able to give and receive it both, graciously. Always remember that no matter how amazing your spouse or life partner is, your friend must have a special place in your life. This applies not just to wedding decisions but also for other habits and lifestyle choices. Taking drugs or alcohol for instance does not have to be based on friendship. Binge drinking usually goes hand in hand with peer pressure.

Always remember that if a friend encourages you to pursue failure and calamity, they aren't your friend.

8

THE 3 TIMELESS TESTS OF FRIENDSHIP

Friends come in all shapes, colors and sizes. Some friends stay with us for life although they may be miles apart and some friends betray us for no apparent reason. As much as we must cherish social bonds, we must be cautious about the people who we rely on.

> *The only way to have a friend is to be one.*
> **- Ralph Waldo Emerson**

It may sound silly to some people to test whether or not someone is worth being a friend but to others it may only seem logical. There are 3 simple ways to know if a person is worth being your friend. These tests do not have a right or wrong answer because you are the best judge of what is right for you. But these situations will help bring out the true colors of your potential friend and assist your decision making and trust building. So here they are:

1- **Tell them a secret**

2- **Travel with them**

3- **Lend them money**

When you **share a secret** with someone and ask them not to pass it around, it makes that person responsible and accountable. If they pass other people's information to you, they certainly gossip behind your back too. If your secret gets leaked, you will know it soon through other friends. You would know how trustworthy this person is.

Travel either for a day or weekend to spend more time with them. When you travel or visit a different place, you can notice if they split the bills, if they leave you alone and get busy with their phone or with other people, how they behave in public, what bothers them, if they are racist, sexist etc. There will be hundreds of unexpected situations that will bring out their real personalities and most probably you will then know if they can be your long term friend or not.

Lending Money is simple and straight forward. Don't lend a huge amount and cry later. Just ten bucks would do. See if they thank you, are they bothered to return it, how long did they take to return it and with what attitude. You may not want it back but it is good to see if it bothers them and if later they try to make it up by offering you a coffee or lunch etc.

These three tests are timeless and classic. They actually come from my grandfather and were introduced to me by my father. Time and again they have proven to be very useful in my life with both genders. I hope you try and find out the true colors of the friends around you.

Section 3

Date Healthy

9
SELF PERCEPTION: YOUR GENDER BOX

Dating is like driving a car in many ways. You cannot look just ahead of you and forget about the other sides. Similarly, dating requires a person to look at all sides of life beginning with the self.

When it comes to relationships, we spend enormous time thinking about the person and criticizing ourselves for eating that last piece of pie or not going to the gym last week or simply for not earning enough etc. We do all this because we are trying to please a potential partner and think that they might chose someone else over us because we are not good enough, smart enough, slim enough, rich enough, educated enough, classy enough and so on and so forth.

What this means is that we are focusing on their needs and giving ourselves hard time for not being able to meet their needs.

However, this is completely ridiculous. If you ever want to have a partner for a few hours or for a lifetime, you must begin with yourself. The perception of yourself for yourself.

You must begin with asking who you are as a person, not as a gender. I lay stress on the gender because that somehow puts you in a box. Let me explain how.

You ask a child what they want to be when they grow up. Their answer would be dreamy and imaginative. You ask a teenager or an adult the same question and their answer would be dictated by everything but their passion. In many countries women are not allowed to pursue education and careers so all they can ever hope to be is a mother and an unpaid maid.

The problem is that as we grow up, our parents, the society, the school and everyone around us place us in a gender box. Don't play dress up and dolls because you are a boy. Don't play football and get dirty because you are a princess, a little girl. Girls are supposed to be pink, delicate, frilly, flowery, fluttering people while boys and supposed to be blue or grey, strong, feeling less, careless and manly people.

> *If a guy is intimidated by a woman in leadership, he has real problems with his own concepts of masculinity. That's a harsh statement, but I believe it to be true.*
>
> **- Tony Campolo**

This doesn't create as much problem for children as it does for adults. Boys grow up with a particular set of assumptions for girls and vice versa. If a girl is not into pink stuff, pretty, lady like then the men she date may feel like she is not the ideal 'wife material' that he can bring home to his mother. Women may feel the same about men who are not like a typical tough guy.

The point here is to **'question your assumptions'** about yourself and the opposite gender. Do you put yourself in the gender box and try to be 'man like' or 'lady like' as the society and media expect you to be? Are you brave enough to show the real you without meeting the superficial expectations of the society? Are you ready to date someone who is not a typical, ideal, cliché of their gender?

Don't use men to get what you want in life. Get it yourself.

-   Helen Gurley Brown

10
NON CREEPY FLIRTING

Today's world of dating isn't going the way your mama and daddy's dating went. Gone are the days of front porch dates that started with a wink at the soda counter and ended with a long night at the drive in, followed by hushed phone calls. In today's world we are engaging with people who we don't know, as opposed to the community atmosphere which gave an aura of protection in the past.

The trick, when you're flirting, is figuring how to keep a balance between being engaging enough to retain someone's attention and not seeming overly available. So you tease a person a little.

- Neil Strauss

Dating safely is incredibly important in this hi-tech digital world. The internet doesn't offer the same safety protections that small communities offered in those days long ago - there's not a community to warn you about people who might wish to harm you, either emotionally or physically. AND you need to know how not to come off as a danger yourself. We do spend so much time meeting and dealing with people in the virtual world, so how do you navigate the real world without looking like a cad? **This book is for people navigating the dating world in the 21st century, who themselves are working through all of the complications that modern life brings.**

> *If I kind of like a guy, then I'm a fantastic flirt. But with a guy I truly like, I get painfully shy.*
>
> - **Shannen Doherty**

During dating there's this amazingly fine line that you must tread between showing too little interest so that the other person thinks you're not interested, and on the other side showing too much interest and crossing that line into unacceptable behavior. Knowing where that line is isn't easy, and teaching you how to negotiate this difficult process safely, with confidence and without coming off as a predator, is what healthy dating is all about.

We feel closer to each other than ever before - hey, I know what you had for breakfast! Saw it on Facebook! But at the same time we're way further away than we've ever been before. There's this crazy thing going on where people feel more comfortable with their virtual friends than they do with their real life compatriots. We're so separated from each other, and that separation is driving a lot of fear.

The world of online interaction means that the boundaries get fuzzy. Where once it was easy to be clear about what was ok on a date and what was over the line, now we have this constant access to each other and suddenly those lines aren't so clear anymore. Be careful with online interactions so that you don't cast yourself as overly eager and therefore dangerous.

Fear is failure, so be without fear. When you're dating, you want to have a comfortable and relaxed feeling. What you don't want is to be ruled by fear - don't have your pepper spray in your hands when you're meeting someone! Dating ruled by fear, either a fear of being personally attacked or even a fear of getting your heart broken, won't lead you to where you want to go.

Never allow someone to be your priority while allowing yourself to be their option.

-Author Unknown

The goal is not to come off as the kind of person who might be predatory. Where does flirting crossover into sexual harassment? It's easy to think that you're just being friendly but to leave your partner feeling vulnerable isn't exactly love or flirting. Being aware of how your actions are understood by the other person is an important part of creating a safe dating environment. If you feel any hint of discomfort in the other person, it's time to back off.

Your endgame is to be comfortable with another person and to allow them to be comfortable with you.

> *If there hadn't been women we'd still be squatting in a cave eating raw meat, because we made civilization in order to impress our girlfriends.*
>
> **-   Orson Welles**

11
NO TRESPASSING- PERSONAL BOUNDARIES

In this chapter, I would like to talk about an actual date situation and discuss what you need to do to avoid trespassing the personal boundaries of your date.

What to talk about

Being a good date is a balance of being a good talker and a good listener. If you have to choose one, choose listener. If the conversation stalls out, look around and find something of interest in the world around you. Maybe the car outside reminds you of your first car. Or maybe the rain reminds you of a favorite book. Whatever it is, look for something that can spark conversation. Some people aren't great at sharing on a first date, so ask questions but don't be intrusive, especially if your date seems shy. Be yourself and be relaxed during conversation, and that will make it easier. Don't ask too personal questions.

> *I used to be a real prince charming if I went on a date with a girl. But then I'd get to where I was likely to have a stroke from the stress of keeping up my act. I've since learned the key to a good date is to pay attention on her.*
> - **Matthew Perry**

Complimenting

So how can you pay a compliment without sounding cheesy, sexist or like a jerk? The answer is by being genuine! If you don't mean it, don't say it. It's got to be true if you're going to make it work. So if you think his shoes are great, then say it! If you think her smile is gorgeous, say it! Don't get overly sexual, and don't worry that it'll sound strange. Dating can be exciting and arousing, so try to keep that in check so that you don't make your date feel uncomfortable. The point here is not to make the person feel smothered or threatened, but rather to show your interest and enthusiasm.

Another great point is to ask a question like - that's a great shirt, where did you get it? Your hair is beautiful, does it run in the family? This shows both that you like something about the other person AND that you want to learn more.

I remember a scene from the famous *Two and a Half Men* show where Charlie Sheen meets a lady who is an attorney. Charlie tries to compliment her by saying "*I did not expect you to be so...so... so.. Yummy*" and then he makes a second attempt and calls her "moist". Poor lady. What Charlie meant was that he was expecting her to look old and haggard while she looked younger than her age.

> *I'm quite sensitive to women. I saw how my sister got treated by boyfriends. I read this thing that said when you are in a relationship with a woman, imagine how you would feel if you were her father. That's been my approach, for the most part.*
> - **Orlando Bloom**

Be careful when you compliment people. When in doubt, please pick up a dictionary or google for suitable adjectives before you start talking.

Table manners

Be polite at the table. Don't double dip with your appetizers. Place your napkin in your lap when you sit down. Chew with your mouth closed. Don't eat too much, but do eat something, At this point I kind of feel like your mother, but we truly forget these things! Think about where you are and what you're doing at the table, and try not to let your mind wander away so that you make horrid table mistakes. Playing with food in a sexy way in an attempt to seduce your date may wither go horribly wrong or rarely right. Make sure you chose the safe path and save the seduction for a later time when you both are more comfortable with each other.

Past and Exes

The rule is that you don't talk about your exes or past relationships on a first date. Period. This introduces a level of baggage and intimacy that your relationship just isn't ready for. So don't do it! most people have some memories of their past and if and when they share it with you, don't be judgmental about it. you may disagree with their life choices or decisions and if you do, please do not try to force them to think your way. A healthy conversation is great but making someone feel guilty or horrible about their choices and being judgmental about their past is one of the worst things you can do. In a stable relationship, this counts as emotional abuse. Be on the watch if someone does that to you.

Ending the evening

Hopefully the evening has gone well and you're ready to set a time for the next date. It's appropriate to hug or even kiss on the cheek on first date if all has gone well. Don't push intimacy further than you feel it should go though. Follow your instincts.

> *Kindness is really important to me in finding my own prince - so are patience and a sense of humor. Without those qualities he's no Prince Charming!*
> - **Anne Hathaway**

Going back to an apartment isn't a great idea on a first date, because keep in mind that this is a FIRST date, and that you in fact don't know this person all that well. It's best to keep your guard up here at the end of the date, because you don't know the exact intentions of the other person. And staying away from the bedroom will make sure that you have time to get to know your partner's boundaries. The temptation to push things can become overwhelming if you put yourself in an intimate situation. Safe dating is about setting yourself up for a positive relationship, and not tempting yourself with situations that invite you to commit actions that you might regret. Finishing up the date in a public place is a great, low pressure way to cap off a wonderful evening.

Bonus: how to get out of a boring date

The courteous thing to do is to muscle through it. Be polite and interested in what the person is saying. Because remember that even if this person isn't your soul mate, they are still a person and deserve respect. And who knows, maybe they have a great coworker who's perfect for you! Life is a web, so this connection might not be the right one but it could lead to the right place.

You can always cut the night short by saying that you're exhausted from work or have an early morning. But they know it's not going well too, so rest assured that they're likely ready to get it over with as well! Don't ever feel that just because there is no long term prospect, why not make it a one night stand and delete them from your phone.

> *"I have no luck with women. I once went on a date and asked the woman if she'd brought any protection. She pulled a switchblade on me."*
> **- Scott Roeben**

13
SEXUAL DOUBLE STANDARDS

One important element of healthy dating is the absence of sexual double standards. Let me tell you a short story here about how I came across the first one in my life.

While I was in Switzerland studying for my MBA degree, I had a friend who was dating a cute Dutch guy. The campus was close to the university and since the campus was small, the students were almost like a close knit community.

My friend and this guy dated for one semester and after the second semester began, he cheated on her with a

Russian girl. Depressed she decided to go away for a while. Since she was an international student like me, she could not travel 10 hours to see her family so she decided to see one of her ex boy friends who was still good friends with her after they mutually broke up.

> *When a man gives his opinion, he's a man. When a woman gives her opinion, she's a bitch.*
> **— Bette Davis**

The moment she was gone, there was a lot of chit chat behind her that I happened to hear. Guys from all countries talked smack about her using derogatory words and the century's old 'slut shaming' thing. I did not get why they talked smack about her and argued that her boy friend cheated on her, why isn't that something bad? As it turns out, he was 'the man' or 'a hero/dude/player/winner' etc for fooling around with women while my friend was infamous because she decided to meet her ex for the weekend.

It doesn't matter what she does with her ex; that is her personal choice and no one should judge her because she is a single woman. On the contrary, a guy is cheered and applauded when he cheats because somehow it shows how macho he is.

> *As long as she thinks of a man, nobody objects to a woman thinking.*
> — **Virginia Woolf,** *Orlando*

If you believe in this sort of BS, then you rather date someone from the 40s because that was the time when this mentality was considered appropriate. Whether you are a man or a woman, you have no right to judge other people's morality when you must be examining your own.

I am not surprised to see this sort of gossip in India because it is a conservative society embedded in patriarchy. However, I was shocked to see how double standards prevail in the Western world too.

The issue here is not men judging women or the other way around. It is about freedom in its true sense. It's like saying if I steal, I do it because I am hungry, and if you steal you are a thief.

You are the best judge to decide what is best for yourself. Whether you flirt or not, have sex or not must be your decision and no matter what you choose for yourself, you must never try to impose that on other people. Slut shaming is a phenomenon where women are humiliated by others for being open about their views or to be honest any number of things; relevant and irrelevant. It is to humiliate a person for whatever the reason. It is a classic example of double standards. In this generation, most people date, flirt, hang out with sexually available partners and want to live their lives exactly the way they want.

Sometimes some people's personal things become public and this is when others begin to shame them as if they are saints. Dating requires understanding on both sides and if you think it is OK for you to have n number of sexual partners but your partner is a slut for having the same number, then you are a hypocrite.

> *The rule seemed to be that a great woman must either die unwed ... or find a still greater man to marry her. ... The great man, on the other hand, could marry where he liked, not being restricted to great women; indeed, it was often found sweet and commendable in him to choose a woman of no sort of greatness at all.*
>
> **— Dorothy L. Sayers, *Gaudy Night***

15
HOOK UP CULTURE

Hook up culture in this generation is referred to as 'hooking up with mostly strangers for one night stand without any commitment or relationship'. It is purely sexual and temporary.

On the internet you will find heated arguments both for and against hook up culture exploding with pros and cons of both sides. I am sure you have already read them or you can find them if you need to. Some claim that hook up culture is empowering for women while others argue that there are extreme double standards because men who do the same are celebrated while women who chose to sleep with strangers are defamed and humiliated. Hence the term 'slut-shaming'.

I want to use this space to inform you the less talked about aspect of hook up culture.

YOU

Do you do things because everyone else does it?

Are you the trend follower or trend creator?

> *If you choose to engage in one night stands, make sure you have a good reason and peer pressure is NOT one.*

No one can tell you what to do. It is you who must decide what you want. If you choose to engage in one night stands, make sure you have a good reason and peer pressure is NOT one.

Growing up some people feel that unless they sleep with n number of people, they would not know what dating and sex is about. This makes me curious and recently I ended up interviewing my friend about it.

She and her partner met when they were 19 and this was the second relationship she ever had. I was curious to know if she ever felt bored or unfulfilling. If she ever thought that she missed out on life because she did not sleep with several guys and if she feels content.

To my surprise, her answer was simple. She said she found early in life what most people find either late or never find at all. I admire them both for being able to believe in each other for almost twelve years of partnership without regrets. They did not give into peer pressure of trying out other people just for the sake of it.

Ultimately we all need happiness from our relationships. Hooking up with people who do not care about your happiness or you; is a serious and big decision. If you do decide to hook up, you must have a good reason for it just as you would to have a relationship. Because no matter how temporary, it is still a relationship.

Yes, relationships are hard work. They are complicated.

Section 4

End Violence

17

BYSTANDER INTERVENTION

Did you know that in a college campus, at a certain time, there always are a handful of people who will commit sexual assault?

When they do commit assault, they will target a handful of victims.

The largest group of people is neither the perpetrators of assault nor the victims; they are the bystanders. Sadly, the truth is that at times of assault the bystanders do not intervene and this is why the numbers of victims is looming in every community.

Thom Harnett said that *"One person speaking up makes more noise than a thousand people who remain silent."*

The word bystander by definition means someone who is a spectator or witness but does not get involved. This is a choice that you and I make.

> *Be an active bystander because sooner or later you or someone you love could be a victim too.*

It does not have to be that way. Be an active bystander because sooner or later you or someone you love could be a victim too. No one today is immune to assault, not even inside our homes. The longer we ignore it and run away from it, the longer it is going to chase us. Like an ugly monster, it has to be confronted.

In this chapter you will learn about bystander intervention; actions you can take to intervene the situation and avoid assault. However, please note that this does not mean that you must put your life at risk. You are the best judge of the situation and only by assessing it, you can judge what steps you must take. If the situation is life threatening, you **must call the cops/security** or raise alarm without trying to be superman.

Assault can be of many types and here we will explore sexual assault, rape, domestic violence and stalking broadly. You might know a friend who is going through a rough relationship and notice signs of physical violence on her/his body. You may know a friend who is crazy about an ex and is trying to spy on that person/ trying to hurt them in some way. You may be in a party where you notice one person absolutely drunk and another person trying to take advantage of their drunkenness. It can be anywhere anytime. So keep your eyes and ears open.

There are 5 steps to follow that might break the situation.

1.   Take notice

Being mindful and aware of your surroundings is the first step. Take notice of where you are, who is around you and what is going on.

2. Interpret it as a problem

Listen to your intuition. If you doubt there is something wrong, check it out. See it as a problem. For instance, if a person is drunk and you see another person trying to take advantage, don't simply judge that they shouldn't have been drunk or they must be responsible for putting themselves up in a situation like this. Just view the situation and ask yourself 'is this acceptable?' If you see it as a problem, then recognize it.

3. Personal responsibility

Many of us do notice our surroundings and even get upset seeing one person trying to take advantage of another. But something stops us. I call it the 'Lucifer'. This Lucifer will whisper in your ear;

Don't worry; it's not your business.
Forget about it, they probably deserve it.
Hey, what are the cops for?

Who cares what happens to this person, I am not related!
May be they don't need help.
Ah, someone else might surely help them, I m too weak.

These are just a few examples of the excuses Lucifer puts in our mind in order to stop us from taking any action even though we have noticed that there is a situation that needs our help.

4. Confrontation or breaking the situation

Now that you have decided that you must help, you must know HOW TO. If you perceive danger of any kind, if there is violence involved or any threat to your safety, please do not put yourself in danger. Just call the cops or security or raise an alarm. You will be the best judge of the situation so decide wisely.

In other non violent scenarios, even when you chose to personally confront the potential perpetrator, you don't have to punch and kick. The point is to distract the people involved.

Go and ask time, making them aware of your presence.

Ask the victim if s/he has friends around.

If you are a friend, just go and start chatting tirelessly and pretend you are mad that they didn't keep their promise to go shopping or somewhere with you.

You can literally think of a thousand creative ways of breaking up the situation and making sure the assault does not turn into rape.

If your friend is the one trying to take advantage of someone, you can play the same game, begin a conversation, tell them their mom is calling, their car has been smashed...etc

5. Get other people involved

If you are in a public place and there are other people around witnessing the assault through the corners of their eyes, just get close to them and start talking to them about it...

Did you notice that person?

Yeah, how tacky, right?

Yeah, we must interrupt I suggest.

Yeah, who knows what this would lead to?

Right, let's just go and ask the victim if they are alright…

This way a simple conversation with others who are worried like you but stopped by the Lucifer, will be able to kick his ass and be an active bystander.

The world suffers a lot. Not because of the violence of the bad people but because of the silence of the good people.

- Anonymous

18
SWEARING, LANGUAGE AND RAPE CULTURE

This chapter is an extension of the bystander intervention in some ways. The focus of this chapter is how we contribute to the assault and rape culture through **our** language and attitudes. This is actually a big picture and you may want to step back and try to see the whole cycle.

For instance, how many times have we all heard an angry person call someone the word used for genitalia? Many of us, right?

Now think of the people who have those genitalia... The word used in a derogatory sense to humiliate someone is an actual part of someone. And this body part is not a choice; it is what they were born with. Is using that particular word really the best way to communicate your anger or frustration over someone?

> *What's the worst possible thing you can call a woman? Don't hold back, now. You're probably thinking of words like slut, whore, bitch, cunt (I told you not to hold back!), skank.*
>
> *Okay, now, what are the worst things you can call a guy? Fag, girl, bitch, pussy. I've even heard the term "mangina." Notice anything? The worst thing you can call a girl is a girl. The worst thing you can call a guy is a girl. Being a woman is the ultimate insult. Now tell me that's not royally fucked up.*
>
> **— Jessica Valenti, Full Frontal Feminism**

Now let's talk about rape jokes. From daily TV shows to our daily lives, we hear them, we laugh at them, we get annoyed by them, we are disgusted by them but we don't usually stop them. Just like I mentioned in the bystander action steps, you have to take personal responsibility and speak up. Make people aware that you are not comfortable with such jokes and that these jokes **trivialize** and **normalize** the most horrific experiences of some peoples' lives as well as **trigger PTSD**. If they really need a good laugh, they can watch those silly cat playing piano videos but to make fun of an assault is not funny at all.

It is not just the words we speak but also the songs we listen to. Pop culture has changed gigantically since last few years and many songs have become much more violent, blood stained and misogynistic. According to The Guardian and several other bloggers, the song *Blurred Lines* by *Robin Thicke* has been tagged as the most controversial song of the decade. The song lyrics as well as the video are criticized. On a superficial level one may argue that there are so many songs out there with vulgar lyrics and virtually naked dancers, why this one got the hit?

The truth is, it is not just about one song. It is about the message it portrays. In this age, when rapes and sexual assault are at the peak, activists and advocates are trying to change the way we **'allow'** that assault to happen. A song that reinforces non consensual sex is actually reinforcing the myth among young men that a woman would not consent because she is trying to appear 'good' or moralistic. Therefore it is alright for men to assume that she wants to have sex.

When it comes to opinions, the social media is full of people who would swear, abuse and use any means possible to silence another surrounding controversies like this. It instantly becomes a **gender war;** men vs women issue and people just argue and defend their gender code blindly rather than examine the reality.

I cannot put words in your mouth or tell you which songs to listen to. No one can. It is only you who must be able to judge the truth from the terrible. We all want to have fun in life, right? Songs that are fun, friends that are fun, activities that are fun… Great! Have fun but not at the cost of someone else's misery. Make sure your fun is not mocking someone's pain and your enjoyment is not another's suffering. The melody of your ears must not be the cries of a powerless.

19
PORN AND YOU

Ran Gavrieli's is the guy who introduced me to the issue of porn first time in my life. I had never heard a man come forward and discuss one of the most taboo subjects with such honesty and simplicity before. Ran is an expert on many issues that the young men and women face but basically how pornography affects them. Ran Gavrieli's keynote speeches focus promoting emotionally and physically healthy sex by eliminating porn.

One of the crucial points of his talk that I would like to reiterate is how porn generates demand for sex trafficking. He says that when one person desires a certain kind of porn, a specific kind of woman for instance, that creates a demand for them. When there is a demand, people create a supply. While prostitution is a legalized profession in many countries, not many women are willing to work for it. Hence, the kidnapping, the coercion, the human trafficking industry all to create a supply.

> *Pornography is "visually magnetic" to the male brain. ...Enough is never enough*
> **-Anonymous**

Prostitution and sex trafficking aside, let's talk about porn and your personal life for a moment. What age were you when you were first introduced to porn? Did you learn about sexual intercourse through a proper curriculum or through a friend or through porn? Most people in this world have not taken official classes on sex education in school. A growing young person however is curious to discover the secrets of adulthood. Finding no other honest and honorable method of discovery, they turn to porn. Once they do, porn becomes a habit. For many, it is an obsession.

Porn- the new Cocaine

Yes, you read it right. Scientists and researchers claim that watching pornography has the same impact on human brain as that of consuming narcotics.

Our brain is the powerhouse of our body and as we know every function of our body is directed from the brain. Our food and drinks have a direct impact on the health of our brain. The average age of exposure to porn for youth is 11 years old. 9 out of 10 young people under 17 watch porn. 30% of addicts of porn are women.

Watching pornography releases certain chemicals and hormones in our brains such as dopamine, epinephrine, serotonin and oxytocin etc. Although these are natural chemicals that your body produces, an overload of these hormones is unhealthy. Watching porn constantly creates an overload of these hormones in your brain and after a while the same imagery does not have the same effect anymore. Or in other words, the same clips and pictures do not turn you on; you get desensitized to them. This leads to you desiring more images and videos creating an endless cycle of desire. To get the same rush as you were used to, you will require not just more of it but also a hard core version of it. Gradually your brain will become dependent on those chemicals and rewire itself to feel that the rush is normal. This is what addiction is. Other drugs such as cocaine and heroin have the exact same impact on our brains.

Hence, porn is extremely harmful and addictive.

Porn and our relationships

The emotional and psychological impacts of porn on our relationships are well researched by social scientists and psychologists. Our brain has these elements called the Mirror Neuron Networks that are similar to those of monkeys. What we see, hear and perceive as children, we consider that to be normal and consciously or subconsciously imitate that in our behavior.

Watching porn make us imitate that behavior in the bedroom. While porn is sex, it is unnatural and unhealthy sex. There are several cuts and takes which make the scenes last as long as the director wants. In real life however, sex cannot last forever. This longer version creates false expectations among partners.

Most pornography is violence against women where the woman is subjected to some kind of torture or domination and the filthier the violence, the more exotic the video. No human being in the world deserves to be used and objectified the way porn videos portray and especially not your own partner. Using hurtful language or actions during sex is not just a temporary thing. It has long lasting effects on your love life. Porn actors act having sex in weird positions and ways which may be physically impossible for a normal woman yet if she is unable to enact that, her partner may feel like he is with the wrong person.

> *The porn films are not about sex. Sex is airbrushed and digitally washed out of the films. There is no acting because none of the women are permitted to have what amounts to a personality. The one emotion they are allowed to display is an unquenchable desire to satisfy men, especially if that desire involves the women's physical and emotional degradation.*
>
> **— Chris Hedges, *Empire of Illusion: The End of Literacy and the Triumph of Spectacle***

The use of hands is crucial in love making. Porn on the other hand does not use a lot of hands since the camera needs a place therefore there is no holding, embracing, hugging, caressing etc which are the most crucial elements of intimacy. Being intimate with a person is not just about a few seconds of orgasm but more about the time spent sharing and feeling each other's skin and breath on our bodies.

False expectations, stale relationships and betrayal are all just few ways in which porn can ruin our private and most valued relationships.

Please note that the impacts of porn are a huge and complex issue. The information I have provided here is just the tip of the iceberg. You may have several questions and arguments in favor of porn which is fine. The purpose of the chapter was to inform the scientific impacts of watching porn not to stop you from watching it. Now that you know about it, you can chose to go either ways but **you can never say that you didn't know.** Your life and your relationships are valuable and what you do with it must be only your choice. So chose wisely.

20

STREET HARASSMENT

Imagine spring is in the air. Its late afternoon and the cool breeze is caressing over the warm crisp grass after a long day. You can smell the bloom in the air and hear the birds sing their way to life. You are peaceful inside, walking down the street noticing the funny shapes of the clouds in the light blue sky gold plated with the butter scotch colored sunlight and then suddenly you hear *"hey sexy, nice thighs... you wanna lift???"*

Walking down the street is the simplest, easiest, silliest thing to talk about but sadly some people have made it a challenge for women to walk down the street in peace without getting harassed. So what exactly is street harassment?

Street harassment constitutes a number of activities including staring, verbal remarks (both derogatory and complimentary), groping, and honking etc with the intention of harassing another person. Usually people assume that women and girls are the only victims of street harassment but that is not true. Transgender people, LGBTQ and even men may be victims of street harassment. However when men get harassed on the street it usually is by other men and therefore it falls under the category of **bullying** rather than sexual harassment.

Getting back to the street harassment faced by girls and women, it is a sad but an interesting concept to me. And that is because of my personal experiences. When I was 18, I had just finished school and faced harassment every single day. While going to school, wearing my school uniform (first a skirt and then a traditional Indian loose trouser and long top also called Salwar Kameez), I would hear cheap remarks from passer bys and see middle aged men blowing kisses in the air while dropping off their nursery kids at the school gate. When I turned 19, I decided to take matters in my own hand and started wearing **hijab.** For those of you who are unfamiliar with the word, it means the complete black gown which shows nothing but the eyes, worn by Muslim women globally.

Wearing Hijab felt empowering because people did not get to see my body parts to comment on them and Muslim men feared inside the hijab could be a woman from their own home. I could go out and run errands without having to drag my dad everywhere for safety. My skin got fairer and healthier since I avoided the Indian scolding sunlight baking my skin. However, the street harassment did not end. **Men could see my eyes, right?** So they would sing songs on my eyes!

Many people argue that women make a big deal out of silly things such as a strange guy complimenting her by appreciating her smile or the way she walks or talks or swears. The truth is, NO, it doesn't feel good to be approved by strange men on the street for being their '**eye candy**'. Moreover, street harassment is not just admiring a strange woman's body... it soon turns to insulting her for rejecting you, then it turns to bullying a woman who is not physically attractive, which then becomes more serious towards younger girls, then groping women's bodies at public places or even flashing your own junk in order to get their attention. It is a slippery slope from the first compliment to the most severe sexual assault that is rape. Nevertheless, we cannot trivialize the smallest of acts and words that make people uncomfortable on the street.

Also note that street harassment and flirting are two absolutely different things. Flirting is mutual; meaning you get a positive response from the person and most importantly, don't try to flirt with every passing woman on the street. It just makes you look like a looser who has nothing to do in life. If you really enjoy flirting and want to pick up a girl, the worst idea ever is to throw cheesy lines on any woman on the street. Please, do yourself a favor and go to a bar or join a dating group, but don't try this on the street.

Many of us see someone being harassed and recognize it yet we don't intervene. We think:

It's none of my business.

I am too busy to get into trouble.

May be they don't need help.

She seems fine, she can handle it.

It's just normal; she must feel obliged to get male attention. Isn't that the whole point of her makeup?

Why did she dress like that; she is clearly asking for it.

I feel bad for her but I am helpless.

I want to help but I don't know how.

We must learn to live with it.

Who cares, dogs bark, just ignore them.

If only I would have a weapon to teach them a lesson.

All these statements are common thoughts of the bystanders who witness street harassment but do not know how to intervene and mostly whether to intervene at all.

Here are a few simple and easy ways to deal with street harassment:

1- **Know what it is.**

You cannot combat a crime when you do not know about it. You must know that words, actions whether or not they involve touching count as harassment. You cannot even stare at someone constantly and get away with it. Street harassment is not just wrong per se but it is also a crime under the law in almost every nation in the world. So, no matter what a person is wearing or doing, the best thing to do is mind your own business.

2- **Questioning your own beliefs.**

While it is easy to object to harassment that others portray, it is easier to pass by our own acts. Begin with yourself. Question your own beliefs about the common courtesy you must extend to others in a public space and notice where you draw the lines. Question if your own acts make people uncomfortable and try to change them.

3- **Being the male ally.**

As the title of this book suggests, be friendly. Be an ally who stands by when needed. This does not mean that the person you have stood by must be your friend or worse that she owes you something because you stood by her. Friendliness is a component of humanity. Be there for humanity.

4- **Challenge sexist and demeaning language.**

Language and behavior of your friends must be challenged when you see it. Don't laugh along. If it bothers you, it must be challenged. Words or attitudes that objectify women as if they are not humans but just body parts or toys to play with. Every human being on the planet deserves respect and when you hear someone violate that respect whether they are present or not; confront them and tell them that they are wrong.

5- **Be wise.**

Challenging your friends is easier than challenging a total stranger or rather a group of strangers harassing a woman. Be safe. If you feel danger, call the cops. You can simply approach to the victim and ask if she is alright, if she needs help without even challenging the strangers directly. This way they would know that someone is there to stand up and probably challenge them if needed.

The key to challenging street harassment is not violence. Most of us assume that ending street harassment is like a scene from an action film where the hero saves the damsel in distress and confronts the villains when they try to attack the heroine. It does sound thrilling but unrealistic in the real world. Practically, speaking up against street harassment is not about being a hero, getting credit points to be in the good books of a girl or a chance to impress anyone. It is about making sure that everyone has the right to enjoy that spring breeze, golden clouds and chirping without feeling uncomfortable.

22
CONSENT: THE BEST TURN ON

With all the talk about sexual assault and rape, one word that we constantly hear is **'consent'**. In layman's terms it simply is the permission that one person gives to another. Sexual consent is when both adults willingly indulge in a sexual activity. I am sure most of us do know that when a person is drunk enough not to be able to drive, they cannot give consent for sex (I really hope that

> *Isn't that just typical. You're either asking for it, or having it forced upon you without your consent. Who decided women always have to be passive in sex?*
>
> — **Nenia Campbell, *Tantalized***

you already know this).

Interestingly enough, it is easier said than done. Asking for consent can be embarrassing and challenging because of the fear of rejection. Instead of asking for consent and getting rejected, many people find it easier to go ahead with their actions and happily forget about consent 'assuming' it was a yes.

After all, as kids we saw the sleeping beauty getting kissed by the prince in her sleep and today we live in a society where assuming consent is easier than asking for it. While most of us enjoyed watching Disney's *Sleeping Beauty,* we never really question whether or not she wanted the kiss. We see this in movies all the time when two people are talking and all of a sudden one person jumps on another with their tongue in the other person's mouth out of the blue. Of course in the movies they make it look passionate, erotic and an unpredictable sexual encounter. Yet in real life, such erratic behavior is very likely to get you a free ride in the police car.

You might be surprised to know that the highest numbers of rape cases that are reported to authorities are acquaintance rapes i.e., the victim is a friend, partner, boyfriend, husband, a member of the family or somehow related to the victim in some way. This is a puzzle for a logical brain because the fact that two people know each other is evidence of a connection between the two. A rapist that comes of the bush in a dark night, does his nasty and vanishes into the dark is never going to ask for consent obviously. But people who we know, we trust and rely on; must be open enough to share their feelings with us and ask if we want to have sex or not. Sadly, the numbers tell that many don't.

> *Convincing someone to have sex is the same as manipulation and does not actually count as getting consent.*

Convincing someone to have sex is the same as manipulation and does not actually count as getting consent. It must be a straight, enthusiastic, flirty, willing, big YES. Sexual intimacy is a beautiful connection between two individuals. It isn't vulgar or cheap or morally degrading. However, forced sex i.e. rape is all those things apart from being a serious crime.

Many of us agree with all these arguments about consent yet we may hesitate to ask for it. Here are some pointers to help you out.

Ask if s/he would like to join you for a coffee/drink.
Ask about his/her likes, dislikes.
Compliment when you genuinely mean it.

Use appropriate language and show respect while complimenting. E.g. "your hair looks lovely, does that run in the family?" or "Your accomplishments are very impressive, tell me more about your work."

When you do get to be friendly enough, **ask** if they would like to meet you again or continue the talk elsewhere. Only if they agree, take them to a place where they ask you to.

Once you are comfortable, **ask** how they feel.
Assuming they are comfortable, **ask** if you can kiss them.

If the kiss goes well, **ask** if they would like to get intimate with you.

If they do say yes, it is easier to begin by talking about sexual preferences.

We all have sexual values and preferences (the least talked about thing of all our conversations).
Once you both know what one another likes, it gets the mood lighter and romantic.

Assuming you do begin the activity, **please, please, please keep asking** if they are alright and if they like it. **I emphasize on asking because silence is not a yes!**

You must know that even if a person agrees to have sex and then withdraws consent in the middle, they are not liable to finish the process and neither do they owe you anything.

The moment they get uncomfortable and want to either stop or pause, you must respect that as well as make sure they respect your wishes.

Consent is all about communication. Since we all know that alcohol has the power to impair our judgment, it is highly recommended to keep your alcohol intake to a minimum in order to remember and enjoy the experience properly.

> *Consent is sexy, yes but most importantly, it is mandatory.*

Many people will get rejected as well when they ask for consent. If you ever get rejected, handle it like a courteous person and move on with your life. Don't take it personal, ever. Every person you are attracted to would not be automatically attracted to you like in the movies. When you do get rejected, pass a smile, wish them well and leave them alone instead of calling them names or making comments like "you are not beautiful anyways". Such demeaning and rude remarks will never give you anything but make you bitter and mean human being.

To end this chapter, I would like you to imagine two scenarios.

- Imagine the person of your dreams right in front of you, whispering in your ear *"I want to kiss you so bad"*.

- Now imagine a person kissing (tonguing) you while you have tears in your eyes.

Which one is a turn on?

24
THE INTEGRITY OF STANDING UP

There are two types of people in this world according to me. **Progressive** and **regressive**. Progressive people are the ones who move forward while regressive people slide backwards.

This book has tons of wisdom that was not available to me when I was growing up and if it were, it would have saved me a lot of heartache and tough lessons. But despite those tough lessons, I kept the progressive person in me alive and decided that until I die, I will keep moving forward. Sometimes I might fly, other times run and many times barely drag myself but it will certainly be in the positive direction.

Whether it is the idea of having multi gender friends and looking out for them, or consent; the impacts of porn or hook up culture. Every topic discussed in this book was to inform you deeper about the ways the world harms many of us and could someday harm you. I don't want you to take every word to heart but I encourage you to dig deeper and find your own way. Explore what works best for you and what ideology or sexual values you want to abide by.

Whether or not you agree with everything discussed in the book; please agree to the universal fact that violation of human rights is wrong and **no human dead or alive** deserves to be mistreated.

Some topics may be closer to you than others. May be you relate more to men who are victims of sexual assault. Or maybe you care about child abuse more. There are so many social issues to deal with and no matter how hard we try; there is only so much we can do. I don't care what you feel passionate about. As long as there is something out there happening that bothers you; go ahead and stand up against it. I am sure you know that people who don't stand up for anything fall for everything.

Whatever your cause, associate yourself with it deeply. In school we are taught to care about the planet and the animals and the people but things usually change when we go to college. As soon as most of us enter university, it becomes a rat race to earn more grades and get better jobs. Eventually when we do graduate, we become occupied with earning money. Then comes the marriage and so do the kids. Our lives fall into a rut.

Since we enter university, we begin to live life in our own little bubble. This bubble is our entire world. We completely and happily ignore the fact that there are other people outside of this bubble of ours who may not have enough food to eat or who may need us to speak up for them. We are so busy making ends meet and impress our so called competitors that we become blissfully oblivious to the poverty, the social and economic issues of our society and blame it all on the government and the corporations.

Sure, it is fun to sit peacefully at your garden after retirement, read the newspaper and discuss how screwed up the economy is sitting on your comfy lawn chair. Well, that can cleanse your mind that you didn't have anything to do with it but it can never cleanse your soul. I believe that each and every single one of us has a role to play like the infinite organisms in the biodiversity. We all have a role to play which is bigger than ourselves. This role need not be heroic or fame hungry rather it is being a social catalyst to the progressive world.

This progressive move begins with you caring for yourself. I often ask my participants a question *"who is the most important person in this world to you?"* Their answers usually consist of parents, partners and siblings. My take on it is different. I say that the most important person in this world is **YOU**. If there is NO you, there won't be them. If you want to care and stand up for your beloved ones, you must first care for yourself.

Any person in the entire world who denies your human rights must be challenged. You will be surprised to know about the emotional, psychological and financial abuse faced by people through members of their own families. Children must suffer neglect and abuse from their parents because *"OMG they gave birth to me, I am their property after all"*. Wives and girlfriends must suffer short tempered husbands because how else would they pay their bills if they don't. Men suffer secretly in silence because they are not 'manly enough' if they reveal their emotional side to the society. Strangers who help us out in our bad times might expect us to 'pay them back' through sexual favors.

No matter how nice a person has ever been to you, if they paid your bills, if they fed you food, if they helped you in any god damn way, even if they **gave birth** to you; THEY DON'T HAVE THE RIGHT TO VIOLATE YOUR HUMAN RIGHTS. Your right to respect, safety, protection, dignity and integrity.

When you do make sure that you stand up for yourself and no one will ever be allowed to violate your rights, make sure you respect the rights of others too. Make sure when you witness someone's rights violated, you stand up and speak up.

Love is joy. Do not convince yourself that suffering is a part of it. - Paulo Coelho

Stand for what is right even if you stand alone.

Great Spirits have always encountered violent opposition from mediocre minds.- Albert Einstein

Look around. You may find a friend, desperately hanging to dear life, waiting for someone to offer the real benefit of friendship; give them a voice when they have lost theirs.

AFTERWORD

Your Next Step...

Rethink whatever you thought about dating, friendship and violence prior to reading this book.

Send me your story to see it published in my next book. Please visit my website or blog to get in touch. Accepted stories will get an Amazon gift card worth 5 USD.

Stories could be on any one of the following topics:

- A time when you or your friend stood up for one another in the face of danger.

- How has your friend impacted on your life?

- A date gone humorously wrong.

- Any other interesting story that you feel relevant.

To **UNLOCK** your special **gift**-

Sexy But Safe Dating

How to identify the warning signs of potential rapists, abusers and psychopaths early in the relationship

Please visit www.safespaceeurope.com

COOL PLACES TO HANG OUT

Safe Spaces on www.safespaceseurope.com

Stop Rape Now on www.stoprapenow.org

Stop Porn Culture on www.stoppornculture.org

White Ribbon Campaign on
www.whiteribboncampaign.co.uk

Campaign Against Domestic Violence on
www.cadv.org.uk

A Call to Men on www.acalltomen.org

Stop Street Harassment on
www.stopstreetharassment.org

Hollaback on www.ihollaback.org

1 in 3 on www.oneinthree.com

Male Rape on www.male-rape.org.uk

ABOUT THE AUTHOR

Awarded Academic Scholar & Violence Prevention Speaker, Shahla Khan, Mentors & Inspires Young Men And Women to Unify Against Campus Assaults, One Campus at a Time.

Shahla Khan is on a mission to unify young men & women in higher education institutes around the world to prevent campus assaults, one campus at a time so education can be safer, memorable and personally fulfilling based on trust, friendship and empathy.

Having overcome her own battle with self blame, PTSD and peer pressure, Khan researched and learnt the core myths around gender crimes to begin a journey to spare other young men and women the atrocity of learning life the hard way. A professional Economics and Business Educator having taught at universities in three continents, Khan is a frequent contributor to local and international media and a proficient blogger.

Khan believes that we need to change our approach towards gender based violence and shift our focus from 'men vs. women' to 'crimes vs. humanity'. This is where transformation in perspective must begin and lead us to a hate free generation.

Currently, she is ending her PhD in Economics in the UK. She loves travel, intellectual conversations and babies.

To find out more, please visit her websites

www.shahlakhan.me

www.safespaceseurope.com

www.authorshahla.wordpress.com

www.1lifefoundation.com